Astrology

A Beginner's Guide to Astrological Wisdom

Table of Contents

Introduction

Throughout its orbit, the Moon appears and disappears from our skies. Sometimes, she pokes her head through heavy clouds, and other times, she's the star of the show on an open, clear night. Every so often, she's even visible during the daytime hours when the sun's light hits her at the right angle, and her presence adds that little bit of magic to our daily lives. With her, the tides rise and fall, slowly invading and retreating from our beaches and shores. Vacationers watch the waters approach where they've set up their umbrellas and towels while fishermen plan out their day according to when the tides will be best for them. The waters of our Earth are under her control, and she's a beautiful commander.

The human population is also affected by the Moon's constant orbit around our planet. Any doctor will tell you that there tend to be more accidents and injuries around the full moon, and patients are typically more agitated around that time as well. There's more violent crime and strange behavior, amongst other things. Our world becomes a more dangerous place depending on where the moon is in her cycle. One study held in 2013 showed that people get 30 percent less deep sleep during the full moon, which may be partly responsible for these occurrences, but modern science cannot provide us with a complete explanation just yet. We also know that there are spikes in certain happenings when there's a solar event, including heart attacks, suicides, strokes, and psychotic episodes.

Knowing that the Moon and Sun *both* have an effect over our day-to-day lives, is it so outlandish to believe that other celestial bodies might influence us? Our planet's orbit and the orbits of the other planets in the solar system all balance each other and create a unique peace that took millions of years to achieve; so, who's to say that Jupiter's location in the sky doesn't change the events and occurrences here on Earth?

Astrology is defined as "the study of the movements and positions of the sun, moon, planets, and stars in the belief that they affect the character and lives of people". Astrologists use precise mathematics and astronomy as tools for predicting what will happen here on Earth, and they can even tell a lot about a person's personality through the position of the planets and stars at the moment of their birth. With a little bit of studying, reading, and an open mind, you can also unlock the secrets of the Universe and use them to your advantage.

When is the best time to start a new business? When is the best time to redownload that dating app that you've abandoned? When should you schedule your vacations, and when should you roll up your sleeves and do some work? Believe it or not, astrology can help you with all of these questions and more. This book is intended to guide you through the basics of astrology, teaching you how to incorporate the rudimentary ideas of it into your daily life while also preparing you for deeper studies should you choose to pursue them. Through this beginner's guide, you'll learn the following and more:

- The history and origins of astrology

- The 12 zodiac signs and the traits associated with them

- More placements such as Moon, Rising, and Lilith

- How to use astrological placements to determine your compatibility with others

- Define planetary movements such as Retrogrades and Returns

- How planetary movements can affect your daily life

- How to use astrology to your advantage

With this knowledge, you will have a steady base of information that will allow you to pick up *any* astrology book with ease and be able to understand it. You will also be prepared to incorporate the basic concepts into your daily routine, so you won't have to wait too long before you see yourself, your relationships, and your life improve! Taking the first step into astrology is extremely exciting, and I can't wait to see what you achieve!

Chapter 1: The Basics

What Is Astrology?

In short, astrology is the study of the movement of multiple celestial bodies such as the Sun, Moon, planets, stars, and even asteroids, with the hope of learning how their positioning correlates to our personalities and the happenings of our everyday lives. It is also used for 'divination', the practice of predicting the future. Many people use astrology as a means of determining their romantic compatibility with someone, the outcome of a big decision (such as a career change), and plenty more. Even though we're going to touch on a few astrologies from other cultures, we will primarily be focusing on a style called "Western astrology". This form of astrology focuses around the 12 Zodiac signs: Aries, Taurus, Gemini, Cancer, Leo, Virgo, Libra, Scorpio, Sagittarius, Capricorn, Aquarius, and Pisces.

When people say that they're one of those 12 signs, such as "I am a Leo," or "I'm a Capricorn," they're referring to their Sun sign. This means that the Sun was positioned in the area of the sky ruled by that particular sign. Over time, many people began using only their Sun sign since that sign is seen as the 'true' self, but most astrologers will agree that this is a highly simplified version of Western astrology. To get a complete view of an individual's personality, one must also look at the positioning of the other planets at the moment of their birth, which gives us what we refer to as the "astrological chart" or "birth chart". Using this chart, an astrologer can give detailed predictions about many areas of a person's life.

Within Western astrology, there are a few different forms of interpretation that all look to achieve a different goal:

- **Mundane Astrology**: Did you know that events, inventions, and disasters have astrology, *too*? Through this form of astrology, people try to predict the outcome of certain events, foresee natural disasters, and more.

- **Interrogatory Astrology**: Through this form of astrology, someone can seek answers to specific questions that they may have about their own lives or the lives of others. It can also focus on events that have happened in a person's life, similar to mundane astrology but on a smaller scale.

- **Natal Astrology**: This is the form of astrology that most people are familiar with and of which we'll cover the most in this book. This form focuses on an individual's birth chart and uses the "Law of Beginnings"; that is, the idea that everything that happens to something is determined during its start. Applied here, that means that a person's life can be seen in the star chart when they were born.

Astrology vs Astronomy

Although these two terms are similar in spelling and pronunciation, they bear *extremely* different meanings. 'Astrology' refers to the study of the planet's positions in order to predict a person's personality, future, or other details about their lives. 'Astronomy', however, refers to the broad study of space. Astronomers seek to learn more about stars, solar systems, and the Universe as a whole, and there typically aren't any divinatory or spiritual qualities to the study.

However, these two fields were only separated from each other in *very* recent history. It was only in the late 1600s, when Isaac Newton proposed theories about how the planets move, that we saw a split in the way we studied space and used different words to describe these studies. Nowadays, people seem to pit astronomy and astrology against one another. They see it as a matter of "religion vs science" and mock astrologers for making their predictions. However, as with many matters in this regard, the two studies assisted one another for much of history. Astronomy, as we know it, wouldn't exist if astrologers didn't push for better technology, science, and mathematics to help them read the stars better and understand what their movement meant for those of us on Earth. Even today, the best astrologers are those who have a deep understanding of astronomy and know how to interpret planetary movements.

The History of Astrology

Although modern research has confirmed the fact that celestial bodies have an impact on our society, astrology is an ancient art. You may be shocked to hear that astrology has been around for nearly 4,000 years, while civilization as we know it has only been around for approximately 6,000 years. This means that astrology has been with us for almost as long as we've been farming, writing, and building houses! Long before we were able to confirm the concepts of astrology with science, our ancestors knew that the movement of the stars and planets *had* to have power, and they sought to define *exactly* what that power was; but with limited technology, how did they know what to look for in their search? What civilization discovered this life-changing wisdom, and how did it spread across the globe? Did astrology differ from culture to culture? And how did astrology change over time, if at *all*?

To answer these questions, we'll go back in time about 4,000 years to the Babylonian Empire.

The Babylonian Empire

In modern-day Iraq, during the second millennium BCE, the civilization of Babylon sat comfortably as the hub of human life in its corner of the world. It was the capital city of Babylonia, and it was buzzing with life. Its people had become so proficient at farming, herding, and irrigating that they were able to focus on some of the finer details of life, such as writing and art. It also housed the mythical "Hanging Gardens", which was described in such mystical and awe-inspired terms that modern historians have to wonder whether it was even *real*. Some believe it was built by the biblical king, Nebuchadnezzer II, and others believe it was nothing more than a legend. The ancient Babylonians also inherited a number of stories that came from their more nomadic ancestors; the tales of 'constellations', the pictures people saw in the sky. Nearly all civilizations had their own ideas of what people, animals, and mythical creatures existed in the stars, but the Babylonians were the first to give them concrete definitions and write them down. It was their imagination and ingenuity that gave us the 12 zodiac signs.

The Babylonians were experts at trigonometry and even developed a method of tracking Jupiter's movements that astronomers still use today. We also still use their techniques for tracking time and studying how the Earth's rotation has changed since the days of their empire have passed.

Through travel, trade, and the passing of time, these concepts eventually made it to the ancient Egyptians. As you may know already, the Egyptians are famous for their precise mathematics and the importance they placed on the Sun, stars, and other celestial bodies. They would develop the Babylonian's ideas even further and create a detailed astrological system called "horoscopic astrology", which utilizes a visual representation of the stars' positions to chart where they were in the sky at a certain moment. We still use horoscopic astrology today, and we have the Egyptians to thank for it, but they weren't the ones who spread the system across the globe. The civilization responsible for that enormous task would be the Greeks.

Ancient Greece

Through his conquest of Asia, which led him through Syria, Persia, Central Asia, and Babylon, Alexander the Great took siege of many of the records and technologies used by astrologers. It wasn't long before they became a regular part of Grecian life. They translated cuneiform, the writing style of the Babylonians, into Greek, and with the translations came all of the knowledge and wisdom of the Babylon people. Alongside the transfer of literature came some people who were willing to educate the Greeks about astrology, such as Berossus, a priest of Bel from Babylon. Somewhere around 280 BCE, Berossus began teaching astrology and some other parts of Babylonian culture to the Greek public.

The Grecian astronomer, astrologer, and mathematician, Ptolemy, would publish a work entitled 'Tetrabiblos' that solidified the Western view of astrology from that point forward.

If you ever get a chance to read this book, you'll notice that most of the details are unchanged from how we see astrology in our modern world. There were, however, a number of details about his view of the Universe that would be corrected with time; for instance, Ptolemy thought that Mars was so dry because of its proximity to the Sun, so he supposed it was the closest planet to the Sun instead of Mercury. However, despite his blunders, Ptolemy was a respected scientist who approached his subject matter with an analytical eye, and his work is still very much respected.

Ptolemy wasn't the only Grecian writer who helped to create the zodiac as we know it. Dorotheus, author of the 'Pentateuch', is also widely credited for modern astrology. We mostly have access to this book through an Arabic translation that was approximately created around 800 AD, and the work is still largely fragmented and perhaps corrupted by translators, but we do know that the piece was *extremely* influential in its time and influenced future astrologers from many walks of life.

The Middle Ages

In the Middle Ages, particularly in Europe, astrology was used in tandem with medicine and was often utilized as a means of treating various illnesses. Each zodiac sign became associated with a specific body part, and bloodletting was performed on that body part according to the time of year. For instance, Pisces was associated with the feet, so a person who fell ill during Pisces season may have had bloodletting performed on their soles and toes! Alternatively, bloodletting may have followed the phases of the Moon. Either way, people during the Middle Ages had their eyes on the stars just as much as their predecessors. These bodily associations are still used to a certain degree in modern times, but to a far less extreme.

Astrology Across Cultures

Although this book is primarily focused on the style known as "Western astrology", the western world doesn't have a monopoly on interpreting the stars! In fact, almost all early civilizations saw pictures in the stars and began interpreting them, though each population saw different images and chose to understand them in different ways. With that said, you may notice a number of shocking similarities! It's worthwhile to gain familiarity with a variety of different astrologies, so let's explore some from across the world.

The Chinese Zodiac

Although the Western zodiac is divided into months (with more detailed readings going into the day, and even the *hour*!), the Chinese zodiac is split into years. Each year is ruled by one of 12 animals that follows a certain order: rat, ox, tiger, rabbit, dragon, snake, horse, sheep, monkey, rooster, dog, and pig. Don't forget that the cycle also follows the Chinese New Year, which is a little bit after the Western New Year, so those born early in the year may find themselves falling under the sign of the previous year!

Although most people are familiar with how an animal rules each year, most people don't know that the Chinese zodiac goes into more detail based on the month, day, and even the *hour* of your birth. Those four periods of time are referred to as the "Pillars of Destiny", and each one is said to determine a certain area of your life. The ruler of your birth year determines society's expectations of you, the ruler of your birth month determines your childhood, the ruler of your birthday determines your married life, and the ruler of your birth hour rules your true identity.

The Chinese Zodiac goes as follows:

- **Rat:** The rat rules the years 1996, 2008, and 2020, as well as the time frame from December 7 to January 5 and the hours 23:00-00:59. The rat represents alertness, wit, and flexibility.

- **Ox:** The ox rules the years 1997, 2009, and 2021, as well as the time frame from January 6 to February 3 and the hours 1:00-2:59. Oxen are persistent, straightforward, and simple.

- **Tiger:** The tiger rules the years 1998, 2010, and 2022, as well as the time frame from February 4 to March 5 and the hours 3:00-4:59. This sign is brave and royal, but also very cruel.

- **Rabbit:** The rabbit rules the years 1999, 2011, and 2023, as well as the time frame from March 6 to April 4 and the hours 5:00-6:59. Those born under a rabbit sign are lovely, kind, and beautiful, as this sign has associations with the moon goddess.

- **Dragon:** The dragon rules the years 2000, 2012, and 2024, as well as the time frame from April 5 to May 4 and the hours 7:00-8:59. The dragon is well-respected in Chinese culture and represents honor, success, and authority.

- **Snake:** The snake rules the years 2001, 2013, and 2025, as well as the time frame from May 5 to June 5 and the hours 9:00-10:59. The snake represents malevolence, mystery, and divination.

- **Horse:** The horse rules the years 2002, 2014, and 2026, as well as the time frame from June 6 to July 6 and the hours 11:00-12:59. Horses are associated with energy, brightness, and intelligence.

- **Sheep:** The sheep (sometimes called "the goat") rules the years 2003, 2015, and 2027, as well as the time frame from July 7 to August 6 and the hours 13:00-14:59. The sheep is gentle, calm, and favored by many people.

- **Monkey:** The monkey rules the years 2004, 2016, and 2028, as well as the time frame from August 7 to September 7 and the hours 15:00-16:59. This sign is noted for its intelligence and resourcefulness.

- **Rooster:** The rooster rules the years 2005, 2017, and 2029, as well as the time frame from September 8 to October 7 and the hours 17:00-18:59. The rooster is seen as the most reliable and trustworthy of the signs since it can be depended on as an alarm every morning.

- **Dog:** The dog rules the years 2006, 2018, and 2030, as well as the time frame from October 8 to November 6 and the hours 19:00-20:59. Chinese culture sees dogs as good omens, so those born under this sign have significant fortune under whichever pillar they fall.

- **Pig:** The pig rules the years 2007, 2019, and 2031, as well as the time frame from November 7 to December 6 and the hours 21:00-22:59. The pig is seen as lazy and sluggish, but it's also harmless, well-intentioned, and can be a sign of wealth.

The Celtic Zodiac

The Celtic people are well-known for their connection to nature, so it doesn't come as a surprise to learn that their zodiac follows the lunar cycle and assigns each person a tree. There are also many animal associations under each of its signs, and they are all either animals the Celts would have encountered on a daily basis or that existed in their mythology, such as unicorns. This astrology is also highly related to the Druid religion, which was a huge part of Celtic life and is also centered around the natural world. The focus on environmentalism makes it a favorite of activists and spiritualists across the world even today, especially those with Irish roots who use it as a means of connecting with their identities.

The Celtic Zodiac, including both the trees *and* animals associated with each sign, is as follows:

- **Birch (also Golden Eagle and White Stag)**: December 24 - January 20. Nicknamed "The Achiever", those born under this sign are noted for their big dreams and ambitions. They are natural-born leaders and are often quite charming.

- **Rowan (also Crane and Green Dragon)**: January 21 - February 17. Also called "The Thinker", this sign houses many natural philosophers and visionaries. They may seem quiet and subdued on the surface, but they are filled with ideas and passions.

- **Ash (also Seal, Seahorse, and Seagull)**: February 18 - March 17. People born under this sign are also called "The Enchanter" and are blessed with a vivid imagination and boundless creativity. Not only are they inspired, but they tend to inspire others as well.

- **Alder (also Bear, Fox, and Hawk)**: March 18 - April 14. Called "The Trailblazer", these folks are adventurous, passionate, and have a knack for getting along with others. Their confidence makes them extremely likable and gives them an edge in social situations.

- **Willow (also Adder, Hare, and Sea Serpent)**: April 15 - May 12. People under this sign are called "The Observer" for good reason. They are intelligent and have an outstanding memory, but tend to keep to themselves and are sometimes insecure.

- **Hawthorn (also Bee and Owl)**: May 13 - June 9. With a nickname like "The Illusionist", it comes as no surprise that the people born under this sign often put forth a facade and pretend to be 'normal' while they're actually very colorful and interesting.

- **Oak (also Wren, Otter, and White Horse)**: June 10 - July 7. Just like the Oak tree, these people are gifted with extreme strength and are nicknamed "The Stabilizer" because of it. They are also very optimistic and nurturing, which makes them very good parents and teachers.

- **Holly (also Cat and Unicorn)**: July 8 - August 4. Also called "The Royal", this is the sign made for the throne. They are ambitious and competitive and might even come across as arrogant, but they're also very kind when necessary.

- **Hazel (also Crane and Salmon)**: August 5 - September 1. This sign is called "The Knower", and they are the academics of the Celtic zodiac. They appreciate order, tradition, and efficiency, which may lead them to come off as pretentious to others, but it's only because of their impressive intelligence.

- **Vine (also Lizard, Hound, and White Swan)**: September 2 - September 29. Called "The Equalizer", these folks have a knack for seeing both sides of a story and are good mediators. They also enjoy the finer things in life, such as wine and art.

- **Ivy (also Boar, Butterfly, and Goose)**: September 30 - October 27. Like the stubborn Ivy, this sign is very tough and is nicknamed "The Survivor" because of it. They are persistent, loyal, and have a strong faith that allows them to overcome obstacles.

- **Reed (also Hound and Owl)**: October 28 - November 24. Called "The Inquisitor", this sign is extremely talented at finding the truth in a situation and banishing away mystery. To achieve this, they are often manipulative, but they also have a high moral code.

- **Elder (also Badger, Black Horse, and Raven)**: November 25 - December 23. The final sign of the Celtic Zodiac is Elder, or "The Seeker". This is a fun-loving sign that lives for entertainment and is always looking for freedom. Despite this demeanor, they're also very intelligent and often have a knack for philosophy.

Chapter 2: Sun Signs

What Is a Sun Sign?

When people ask you for your zodiac sign, they are essentially asking for your Sun sign. This represents where the Sun was located in the sky during the moment of your birth, and it shifts once a month. Our Sun signs represent our true selves or a 'default' state of being. If you were asked to describe the core elements of your personality, your description will most likely suit the traits of your Sun sign. As Grant Lewi, author of "Astrology for the Millions", worded it, "You may think, dream, imagine, hope to be a thousand things, according to your Moon and your other planets: but the sun is what you are, and to be your best self in terms of your sun is to cause your energies to work along the path in which they will have maximum help from planetary vibrations." What he means is that our Sun is the boss of our chart and will direct our movements. If we want to change ourselves for the better, we have to work *with* our Sun sign, not against it.

With that said, it's important to remember that our Sun placement is not the only one in our charts. Many beginners get discouraged if they read their Sun sign and find that it doesn't suit them, but they forget that there are many more placements that could affect the way their Sun sign presents itself. Perhaps your Moon is particularly dominant, or you lean heavily into your Rising sign. And, even if you *do* identify strongly with your Sun sign, it's still important to understand the rest of your chart so you can comprehend the complexities of yourself and your life path.

The Sun Signs

Aries

- March 21 - April 19
- Element: Fire
- Symbol: The Ram
- Ruling Planet: Mars

If you were born between March 21 and April 19, your Sun sign falls into the realm of Aries, the Ram. You might be a little thrilled to know that you're the first zodiac in the cycle; Aries loves to go first! They're adventurous, fun-loving, impulsive, and easily bored. If you need help getting a project off the ground, you'll definitely want to put an Aries on the team. They'll throw themselves wholeheartedly and fearlessly into everything they do, and they'll be extremely eager to prove that they were the best fit for the job. They're also extremely good at staying optimistic, energetic, and confident in the face of obstacles. On the negative side, however, they are sometimes uncaring, impatient, and can let their emotions cloud their judgement.

In their interpersonal relationships, Aries personalities are straightforward and simple. They'll tell you what they want, and they like when their partners, friends, and family members do the same. They're extremely loyal and love having close relationships, but those who associate with them *must* be prepared to endure their mood shifts and impulsivity. They will also have to understand that an Aries *isn't* trying to be bossy; that's just how they communicate, and they may have to be reminded to be gentle.

Once an Aries matures, they can be extremely effective leaders, speakers, and teachers. They may also thrive in a career that allows them to channel their bravery and their instinct to be a hero, such as firefighting, armed forces, martial arts, paramedics, stunt person, or even athletes.

Taurus

- April 20 - May 20
- Element: Earth
- Symbol: The Bull
- Ruling Planet: Venus

The second sign of the zodiac, falling between the time frame of April 19 - May 20, is Taurus. Taurus is the Bull, but don't picture a bull rampaging in a china shop! Instead, picture a bull sitting in a calm field, surrounded by yellow flowers, and not having a care in the world. Taurus is a relaxed and stable sign that values traditions, dependability, and practical skill. They also have a *huge* appreciation for physical comforts, whether that means tasty foods, high-class drinks, clothes, or a beautiful home. At their best, they're very relaxing to be around. At their worst, however, they can be stubborn, overly attached to their material possessions, and respond very poorly to criticism.

In their social lives, Taurus values people who can give them consistency and make them feel safe. They have a very serious approach to love and are likely to seek someone with whom they would want to start a family, but they make friends very easily and don't have a hard time being in anyone's company. It takes a while to make a Taurus angry, but once they get there, they can be quite destructive and may break a few hearts. Someone who wants a relationship with a Taurus must be observant of the signs of their anger and be able to address the issue quickly before things spill over.

Since they value stability so strongly, a Taurus would most likely pursue a career that is already well-established and would give them a steady income. They may also enjoy work where they can use their hands or that involves the care of valuables. For instance, they may be drawn to a career as a banker, art dealer, construction worker, financial planner, or a building tradesman.

Gemini

- May 21 - June 20
- Symbol: The Twins
- Element: Air
- Ruling Planet: Mercury

Imagine a Twitter personality or famous YouTuber, complete with all of the funny quirks and controversial content, and you've already gotten the gist of Gemini! These people are humorous, perceptive, unreserved, and are social chameleons. If they're naturally introverted, they're good at pretending to be extroverted, and vice versa. They thrive in social situations and are great for any group project or presentation that requires speaking, quick-thinking, persuading, or charming. If you're in need of help on a project, then a Gemini is definitely the person to turn to. However, Geminis are often afraid of being alone and need to practice enjoying their own company. They can also struggle to express their true emotions, take responsibility for their actions, and slow down to smell the roses.

In love, the Gemini falls fast and hard. They typically find the idea of romance quite appealing and are naturally curious about other people, so they'll want to get to know the cutie across the bar and are socially competent enough to make that first move. They may fall out of love just as quickly if the relationship gets boring, however, so it's important to keep things spicy.

Friendships tend to last longer for the Gemini but may not be especially deep. They're the type to have a large number of friends but very few people with whom they're comfortable talking about their feelings.

A Gemini would *definitely* want a career where they work with other people. Sitting alone in an office would drive them *completely crazy*! Many Geminis also have a talent for technology and gadgets, so they may want to incorporate that into whatever job they choose. Some good careers for a Gemini might be communications, public relations, entertainer, fundraiser, salesperson, DJ, journalist, or computer programmer.

Cancer

- June 21 - July 22
- Symbol: The Crab
- Element: Water
- Ruling Planet: Moon

If Aries is the "adventurous child" of the zodiac, then Cancer is the "worried mother". People born between June 21 and July 22 tend to be sensitive, anxious, and extremely empathetic. They are some of the deepest feelers in the zodiac, and they are easily moved by pieces of media, stories told by their friends and family, and even a beautiful song. They typically care very much about the people around them and have a desire to make a positive influence on the world, which may lead them to caretaker positions. Yet, Cancers are often saddled with melancholy and can be overwhelmed by their anxieties. They are poor at handling change, are bad at receiving criticism without taking it too personally, and are prone to burnout because they feel so much all of the time.

Because of their interest in helping others, relationships are extremely important to Cancers, whether they're romantic, familial, or platonic. They fall in love with the idea of a person as well as the idea of being in love. They may struggle with feeling inadequate in the early stages of romance, but once they've settled in, they'll be in love for the rest of their lives. This makes them vulnerable to returning to their exes or staying in toxic friendships. Still, they can be extremely loyal and helpful companions.

Choosing a career is tricky for the Cancer; they want to help others, but most are too shy to have a job where they interact with people directly. Those who are more extroverted will certainly be drawn to positions like nursing, counseling, and therapy, but others will seek out jobs that are more relaxed. Cancers are extremely good at writing, housekeeping, social work, cooking, gardening, and curating.

Leo

- July 23 - August 22
- Symbol: The Lion
- Element: Fire
- Ruling Planet: Sun

Like the lion, a Leo is bold, loud, proud, and confident. These are the people you see dressed in their best, walking with a bounce in their step, and keeping their nose up to the sky. Leos love to have the spotlight, and their natural charm makes it easy to grab the attention of those around them. They're more than just a walking celebrity, though; Leos are also known for their love of growth and improvement, so they're always looking for ways to better themselves as well as their workplaces, homes, and relationships. If you want someone to help you edit and improve a project, a Leo should *definitely* be your first pick! However, you'll need to be prepared for a lot of bragging, bossing around, and plenty of harsh words. A Leo may even try to steal credit from you as an attempt to look more important!

Flirting with a Leo is just a matter of tossing a few compliments their way and making them feel like the most beautiful person in the room. They'll love someone who can match their energy and help them feel secure in their power. Leos are very prone to loneliness and prefer to surround themselves with people, so they're bound to have a lot of friends in their lives as well. They have what it takes to be generous and loving friends, and they love to be helpful to those in their personal circle.

Leos like a lot of variety and spontaneity in their lives, so they're unlikely to enjoy a career that keeps them still. They'd prefer to be in a more creative or social position. They might thrive as an actor, athlete, hairdresser, event coordinator, interior designer, fashion designer, or talent agent.

Virgo

- August 23 - September 22
- Symbol: The Virgin
- Element: Earth
- Ruling Planet: Mercury

Perfectionistic, orderly, and rational; that's Virgo in a nutshell. These people seem to have their lives together and are unaffected by distractions such as emotion. Of course, that's not entirely accurate; they *do* have emotions, but they often find them baffling and have no good way of expressing themselves, so they turn to the things that make more sense to them. Virgos aren't just obsessed with keeping their own lives orderly; they'll also go out of their way to help others become more organized as well. Some people may find this helpful, but others will think that it's overstepping, so Virgos have to be careful. Still, they enjoy feeling useful and find that it's a good distraction from their feelings of anxiety, imperfection, and self-hate.

Virgos are famously good-looking, and many people find their orderliness attractive, so it's very easy for them to find romantic partners. However, it often takes them a while to *actually* fall in love since they struggle with giving themselves away to emotion, and many struggle to put their criticisms of others aside for long enough to let themselves develop a crush. They're also very particular about the friends they make, but are extremely good at giving advice, keeping secrets, and being supportive in difficult times.

Virgos have *extremely powerful* work ethics and are good in positions that require a lot of training, skill, and dedication. They're willing to put in a lot of effort to whatever career they choose, and they often place their career in the center of their lives. They may feel drawn to accounting, consulting, dentistry, mathematics, editing, or nursing.

Libra

- September 23 - October 22
- Symbol: The Scales
- Element: Air
- Ruling Planet: Venus

Libra's symbol is the scale of balance, and the concept of balance is seen *everywhere* in their lives. This actually makes the Libra a little bit hard to interpret sometimes; they are both introverted and extroverted, proud and humble, loving and harsh. However, this mix of traits is where the Libra can be understood the most if you know where to look. They are empathetic and are capable of reflecting the attitude that people give them, which leads to their mix of traits. They also want to be seen as charming, so they are willing to act as whatever personality they think would be most likable in any given situation. They also value positivity to such a high degree that they have a hard time dealing with negative emotions. In order to grow, the Libra must learn how to handle confrontation, deal with negativity in a healthy way, and enjoy their own company. Life cannot always be the way they idealized it in their heads.

Libras are often regarded as the most beautiful zodiac sign. Not only that, but they think everyone else is beautiful, too, so finding a partner is a simple endeavor for them. However, they will have a hard time opening up to their partner because they fear being seen as too much of a downer, so their soulmate is someone who can support them as they learn to be themselves.

Libras can sometimes struggle in the workplace because they aren't good at handling conflict, but that doesn't mean they don't have talents to show the world. They have an eye for beauty and are amazing in careers that include painting, designing, or styling. They're also good at handling the public, so they might feel called to customer service.

Scorpio

- October 23 - November 21
- Symbol: The Scorpion
- Element: Water
- Ruling Planet: Pluto

The inside of a Scorpio's mind is *ruthless*. They view the world in terms of survival: eat or be eaten, gain allies to increase your odds, take down any threats before they become a problem, etc. They can be social manipulators, kings of gossip, and expert liars. Scorpios usually have a large social group because they're very skilled at getting people on their side and are often very legitimately loyal to the ones they care about, but they're prone to loneliness because their worldview is so unkind. They also love being in control of *any* given situation and may struggle with letting go of that control. All of the manipulating and scheming is just a way to give the Scorpio the empowerment they need to feel happy and complete in their lives. Yet, they are extremely brave, creative, and charming, so they have plenty to be proud of on their own.

In love, the Scorpio goes all-or-nothing. They either don't fall at all or are head over heels, and the difference lies in whether or not their partner can convince them to open up and surrender control. You have to hold the Scorpio's interest and know how to play their games while also taming them, which can be difficult, but also a fun challenge for those who can handle it. In their friendships, Scorpios are deeply caring and compassionate.

Scorpios are good at handling difficult jobs because they're naturally tough. They would thrive as a police officer, doctor, surgeon, rescue worker, undertaker, butcher, paramedic, or entrepreneur. They may also enjoy work that includes fine details, such as analysts, computer programmers, and financial consultants.

Sagittarius

- November 22 - December 21
- Symbol: The Archer
- Element: Fire
- Ruling Planet: Jupiter

A Sagittarius approaches reality the same way someone might approach an open-world video game. There's plenty to explore, multiple skills to master, and *tons* of side quests. A Sagittarius is *definitely* going to aim for a completionist playthrough; they want to try everything, learn everything, and become the best version of themselves. They aren't afraid of change and seem attached to nothing. They don't have a strong concept of 'home' when their home is within themselves, which can be a huge advantage if they ever need to move or travel. However, it can also be a weakness. Sagittarius has a hard time focusing, seeing past their optimism, and keeping their goals realistic. They're vulnerable to heartbreak, danger, and financial struggles because of their occasionally poor life decisions, but those who are close to them know that Sagittarius simply wants the best for themselves and will not settle.

The Sagittarius is often very extroverted and emotionally open, so falling in love comes easily to them. They love people who can keep the relationship exciting and thrilling, as well as someone who is independent enough to endure their many changes. In their friendships, they sometimes have a hard time maintaining a consistent friend group and find themselves jumping around multiple social circles, but they enjoy having many friends and may be especially close to one or two people.

Nine-to-five jobs are absolute *torture* for the Sagittarius! They need freedom and independence in their careers, and they may not want to deal with the public since they can often be *too* blunt. However, they thrive in positions where they can display a skill or make use of their knowledge. For instance, they may enjoy animal training, publishing, writing, religious work, lecturing, interpreting/translating, or personal training.

Capricorn

- December 22 - January 20
- Symbol: The Sea Goat
- Element: Earth
- Ruling Planet: Saturn

Capricorns move through the world in a straight line. They know *where* they are, they know where they want to *be*, and they know *how* they want to get there. They are structured, disciplined, logical, and organized. Capricorns give their all to their work and are always chasing success. Ultimately, their structured lifestyle is motivated by a deep-seated fear of failure. They have a *very* clear idea of what it means to be successful and are extremely anxious about not reaching that milestone, so they work day-and-night to achieve everything that they feel they have to in order to meet that goal. Many Capricorns also prefer to be the ones in control, which is why they work so hard. They want to be the boss, *not* the employee, and they know it takes a lot of effort to get to the top. Their workaholic tendencies can make them very lonely people, and they might struggle to loosen up.

Love can be complicated for the Capricorn, especially if romance isn't on their to-do list. They don't fall in love easily, as they prefer to move slowly once they're in a relationship, and they can be a bit awkward. They would need an independent partner who is willing to endure those snail-paced speeds. Once in a committed relationship, however, Capricorns can be devoted lovers. In their friendships, Capricorns are equally reliable.

With their determination to succeed, Capricorns can excel in *any* career they choose. They're often talented in business, engineering, music, administration, banking, politics, and science. Whatever career they choose, they will likely be aiming to climb the ladder and land themselves in that CEO position.

Aquarius

- January 21 - February 18
- Symbol: The Water Bearer
- Element: Air
- Ruling Planet: Uranus

Aquarius exists to spice up our lives and throws a wrench in what we consider 'normal'. They are contrarians, and they like to take the road less traveled just to prove that it's possible. It's also a great way to stand out, and they might enjoy the attention! Aquarians often take a scientific approach to their decisions and treat life like a social experiment. What will get the biggest reaction? How crazy does a sentence have to be before people start noticing? There's a certain level of curiosity and intelligence to their mindset. Above all, they crave freedom and don't want to be weighed down by things like expectations, responsibilities, and even emotion. That's right; some Aquarius people struggle to handle their deeper emotions because they feel it holds them back. Their free-spirited nature also becomes a problem in structured environments like school and work.

Aquarians might find the idea of a committed relationship a bit intimidating and restraining, but the right partner will know how to navigate this. They need someone who is relaxed, but interesting and who can give them space when they need it, but still keep them invested in the romance. Their friendships are often surface level; they're a lot of fun at parties and events, but may not be the people you go to in a crisis.

Career is a difficult subject for the Aquarian. They really struggle in a nine-to-five, and they *hate* working alone, so it's important for their job to be people-oriented and very exciting. They may be drawn to activism, peace corps, social work, law, psychology, and astronomy.

Pisces

- February 19 - March 20
- Symbol: The Fish
- Element: Water
- Ruling Planet: Neptune

If Aries is the 'child' of the zodiac, then Pisces is the 'elder'. Regardless of their age, the Pisces tends to have an old soul and often bear a very sensitive view towards life. They are filled to the brim with empathy, kindness, and wisdom. They are, however, plagued by anxiety and have a lot of self-esteem issues. In a world that considers soft personalities weak and boring, the Pisces might doubt that they're likable or that their traits are helpful to society at all, and those insecurities may show themselves in the form of social awkwardness or a soft voice. Still, Pisces approaches the world with a sense of wonder and imagination. They are extremely apt at daydreaming and might consider themselves artists, and they may even pursue a creative field of work.

Pisces can be extremely romantic and will fall in love with someone who's willing to go old school. If you're flirting with one, try writing a letter, sending them flowers, or putting a flower in their hair. They may be hesitant to initiate a relationship, but a more dominant partner can be a great fit for them. Pisces find it a lot easier to make friends and can be great for advice and comfort.

Pisces can succeed in a number of creative fields such as photography, writing, dancing, acting, painting, and sculpting. They may also feel called towards a position where they are able to help others and make use of their immense empathy, such as counseling, animal rescue, massage therapy, nursing, or senior care.

Chapter 3: Moon and Rising Signs

Together with the Sun sign, the Moon and Rising signs make up the "Big 3". Instead of introducing ourselves with just our Sun sign, we should really begin by informing people of our "Big 3" to give them a more complete idea of our personalities and lives. More and more people are beginning to do so already. On social media profiles, you'll probably see descriptions such as "I'm a Leo Sun, Sagittarius Moon, and Capricorn Rising." A description like this will tell you three things about a person: their basic personality, the way their emotions manifest, and how they are usually perceived. Let's learn how to interpret the rest of the "Big 3".

What Is a Moon Sign?

Similar to the Sun sign, your Moon sign is determined by the placement of the Moon at the time you were born. The Moon is associated with emotions, feelings, and the ways that we comfort ourselves. Do you ever feel like a completely different person when you've been swept up by emotion? Do your personal habits change when you're feeling depressed, anxious, or burnt out? Do you turn to creature comforts that may be opposed to your overall goals or lifestyle? During those times when our emotions rule us, that's when we see our Moon sign clearly. Knowing someone's Moon placement is a good way to tell how they'll behave when they get upset, and it may even give you some hints about their specific pet peeves and the sorts of things that will get on their nerves. They can also tell you what will be most helpful when the individual gets emotional. Moon signs may also be a good indicator of how someone acts when no one else is around, or how their inner circle might view them.

The Moon moves around the sky at 13.5 degrees per day, making it the fastest of any of the celestial bodies. In comparison, Mercury moves about one, and Mars moves at about 0.5. With its speed, this means that it moves from sign to sign approximately every two or three days. Someone who was born just five days after you will have a completely different Moon sign!

The Moon Signs

- **Aries Moon**: If you have an Aries Moon, your emotions are pretty extreme. You can be impulsive, passionate, and excitable when you're vulnerable and you might even feel a bit childlike at heart. You can be a bit immature at times and might even have mini temper tantrums when things don't go your way.

- **Taurus Moon**: People with a Taurus Moon have fairly stable emotions and are slow to feel the extreme emotions like anger. In times of stress, however, they might turn to creature comforts, material objects, or retail therapy. They might also lose energy quickly when the pressure is on, so they're often accused of laziness.

- **Gemini Moon**: If you're a Gemini Moon, you have an easy time expressing your feelings through language. Keeping a journal or blog might be beneficial to you, especially if you need a place to vent. You may also be the type of person who is quiet at first, but becomes quite talkative once they are comfortable around someone.

- **Cancer Moon**: A Cancer Moon depends on personal security to keep their emotions steady and may be prone to anxiety. They also might adopt a lot of Cancer's natural tendency to give, so they're prone to burnout if they give too much of themselves without getting anything in return. Cancer Moons are also homebodies, so they have to be careful not to isolate themselves in times of stress.

- **Leo Moon**: Leo Moons tend to feel very connected to their emotions and have no trouble sitting with their emotions and working things out for themselves. If isolated, however, this willingness to introspect can turn into egocentrism and drama, so they have to keep their outbursts in check. If they do this successfully, they are generally happy and upbeat people.

- **Virgo Moon**: Virgo Moons are very likely to overthink a situation and give themselves anxiety, which might make them come across as sensitive. To help release those emotions, they can use their solid communication skills to talk to a friend, journal about their thoughts, or engage in self-talk through meditation.

- **Libra Moon**: If your Moon falls in Libra, you may find that your emotions are untouchably secure. You are typically very balanced and are good at keeping your cool in high-stress situations. However, when you're pushed, you might become passive-aggressive and lash out at the people you think are responsible for making you feel that way.

- **Scorpio Moon**: If your Moon is in Scorpio, you will likely adopt some of Scorpio's mysterious qualities, as well as its emotional distance. You struggle to relate with others, it takes you a while to open up, and you might find yourself getting 'stuck' on difficult emotions and it takes a while to move forward.

- **Sagittarius Moon**: The Sagittarius Moon is blunt, straightforward, and direct with its emotions. If this is you, then you aren't afraid of feeling things deeply, and you *especially* aren't afraid of letting others know what's going on inside your head, which is helpful in many situations, but may come across as inappropriate in others.

- **Capricorn Moon**: The Capricorn Moon feels that their career plays a huge part in their emotions. They take things that happen at work very personally, and they need a good work-life balance to feel good about themselves. They also have a very serious and objective approach to emotions in general.

- **Aquarius Moon**: An Aquarius Moon may prefer to focus on their visions, goals, and ideas than their emotions. Because of this, their peers may consider them aloof or even a bit cold, but that doesn't mean they can't connect with people. They simply connect through logic rather than feelings.

- **Pisces Moon**: Pisces Moons are extremely emotional and are deeply connected to their inner lives. They are dreamers, spiritualists, and sometimes even have psychic gifts. They also may resort to escapism and maladaptive daydreaming when they're stressed, so they should focus on grounding themselves when they notice themselves slipping from reality.

What Is a Rising Sign?

While our Moon signs represent our inner selves and our emotions, our Rising sign describes our outer selves. If someone were to guess your zodiac sign off of their first impression of you, they'd be likely to guess your Rising sign rather than your Sun sign. This is the persona you put on in public, the mask you wear at work, and the role you play at parties. Some people may not notice themselves slipping into their Rising persona at all while others may find that they relate heavily to their Rising sign and spend a lot of time there. It all depends on the person! Your Rising sign is also considered the most influential on your physical appearance, though the other signs in your chart may have an effect. We'll discuss how each Rising sign looks and acts in order to get a full understanding of how it works.

This sign is determined by whichever zodiac is on the horizon at the time of your birth, hence why it's called the 'Rising' sign or sometimes the 'Ascendant' sign. This sign changes very quickly, so it's important to know your *exact* time of birth when you calculate your natal chart.

The Rising Signs

- **Aries Rising**: An Aries Rising has a powerful presence when they enter a room. They might come off as a bit intimidating or unapproachable, and they might even seem a bit confrontational or opinionated. They probably look young and have bright eyes. Although the Aries Rising often struggles with hormone imbalances in their youth and teenage years, they typically grow into their appearance later in life and age very well. Their style will range anywhere from athletic wear, to streetwear, to grunge, and they look best in warm and dark hues.

- **Taurus Rising**: Taurus Risings are superb at interviews because they give the impression of being strong and dependable. People feel that they're trustworthy, and although they may seem fierce, they do not seem unkind. Thanks to the influence of Venus, a Taurus Rising is typically very beautiful and has a very nice body, whether it's curvy or sculpted. The lower half of their face is usually very prominent, so they may have round or rosy cheeks, a nice jawline, or plump lips. They might enjoy boho or country-chic clothing.

- **Gemini Rising**: Whether or not they're actually extroverted, the Gemini Rising seems talkative, energetic, and upbeat on first impressions. They might put up a happy facade in order to achieve this effect, or maybe they just amp up the energy when they're meeting new people. Gemini Risings are typically slender and may have broad shoulders, and their hands are usually very attractive. They might enjoy accessorizing their hands and wrists to help draw attention to them. Gemini risings usually dress for the occasion, but lean towards casualwear, simply chic, and lively colors when they can dress however they want.

- **Cancer Rising**: Cancer Risings come off as gentle, warm, and soft-spoken people. On first glance, they definitely seem like the nurturing type, whether they actually *are* or not! They're probably shy around strangers and might take a while to warm up. Cancer Rising women typically look very feminine while the men are well-groomed and may have a soft style. They're especially known for having big, round eyes and naturally long eyelashes. Their beauty is somewhat doll-like, and you may be able to tell from looking at them that the Moon's influence is very powerful. They probably prefer business casual or preppy clothing and look best in neutral to cool tones.

- **Leo Rising**: Like their fellow fire sign Aries, a Leo Rising leaves a strong first impression and makes everyone think that they are confident and fun. They like to appear as vibrant, exciting individuals, and they likely attract a lot of attention at parties. They might even use social media, blogs, or vlogs as a way of cataloguing their eventful lives in a public way. Physically, a Leo Rising has a certain glow about them. This is due to the Sun's influence. They probably have a notable posture that makes them stand out in a crowd, and their torsos are particularly attractive; the women usually have an hourglass shape while the men have muscular backs and chests.

- **Virgo Rising**: Virgo Risings are the sorts of people who simply look like they have their lives together. They seem organized and put-together, so other people may come to them for advice very early on in a relationship. Mercury's influence gives them a very sharp and clean physical appearance as well. They often look very youthful and are drawn to minimalistic fashion such as sophisticated chic or "Sex and the City" vogue. This placement is known for having a prominent upper half of their face, such as well-defined brows or a shapely forehead.

- **Libra Rising**: Regardless of their true nature, a Libra Rising always seems sweet, charming, and agreeable.

They can wrap a whole room around their finger in moments because of their pleasant aura, and this gives them a lot of power in a social situation. As another Venus-ruled sign, they bear a lot of physical similarities to the Taurus Rising. Their faces and bodies are usually very symmetrical and have a beautiful nose and smile. They also have a very attractive lower body. The Libra Rising probably dresses in classy fashion, but they may also enjoy streetwear or cute-comfortable styles.

- **Scorpio Rising**: When a Scorpio Rising enters a room, they are perceived as mysterious, alluring, and sometimes a bit unapproachable. They sometimes attract a lot of attention from those who are nosy and curious, and sometimes they are completely avoided because they've scared off those who might otherwise be interested. The Scorpio Rising is famous for having deep eyes and a cute nose, which gives them an interesting and overall attractive face. Pluto, their ruling planet, governs the pelvic area, so both men and women alike have wide or chiseled hips. They probably enjoy fashion and may lean towards sophisticated-sexy, casual-grunge, or rocker-chic.

- **Sagittarius Rising**: Similar to the Gemini Rising, the Sagittarius Rising gives the impression of being extroverted and bubbly when they first meet someone. They seem excitable, fun-loving, and optimistic. Even when they're just walking around the store, strangers likely note the pep in their step. This is partly due to their physical appearance as well. The Sagittarius Rising usually has long, shapely legs as well as notable hips. They're said to have naturally beautiful teeth as well, which makes their smile very pleasant. A Sagittarius Rising is probably very interested in fashion and likely enjoys athleisure, classy boho, and streetwear.

- **Capricorn Rising**: The Capricorn Rising understands the importance of first impressions and is usually very prepared when they know they're going to meet someone new. Their effort pays off; strangers assume they are responsible, mature, driven, and intelligent. Physically, these signs tend to look a bit like Morticia Addams, complete with the witchy hands and the intelligent but sexy aura. Their hair is usually very thick and dark, and they typically have more body hair than most. Styles such as sophisticated-sexy and casual-grunge suit their dark but smart personas.

- **Aquarius Rising**: Whether they try to or not, the Aquarius Rising *always* stands out. Something about them seems unique and draws the eye. Perhaps they dress themselves in a flashy way, they're unafraid of singing or dancing in public, or they just carry themselves in a way that signals to others that this is an individualistic, innovative person. This sign seems to closely resemble characters such as Phoebe from 'Friends'. They are often blonde and pale, or pale in comparison to the rest of their families. They are usually drawn towards yellows and blues and wear those colors often, and they aren't afraid of being particularly expressive in the fashion they choose. Eclectic styles are *definitely* their specialty.

- **Pisces Rising**: The Pisces Rising has a dreamy, *otherworldly*, sort of look to them. They carry themselves in a light, airy way that makes it seem like their head is in the clouds, though they also seem very compassionate, kind, and thoughtful. They probably seem quite reserved at first, as well. People with this placement usually have very large, vibrant eyes that might be a little wide-set and hair that appears to be windswept. Since Neptune rules the feet, they might be shoe fanatics or love having pedicures. They probably like styles such as boho-lax, athleisure, or even vintage styles such as 80s jock.

Chapter 4: More Placements

Outside of our "Big 3", we may find ourselves influenced by the presence of other celestial bodies and astronomical concepts. Sometimes, we are even affected by comets and asteroids! To understand the rest of the placements, we simply need to know what each planet or celestial body symbolizes, and then we can interpret its message based on what sign it is.

Planetary Placements

Mercury

Mercury, the ruler of Gemini and Virgo, symbolizes the intellect, mind, reasoning, and language. Wherever this planet lands on your chart, it can give you some insight as to what sort of intelligence you bear. Do you express yourself more clearly through writing, art, or music? Do you do your best in your science classes, or do you shine in math? Mercury helps us determine all of these things, so if you're struggling to find your niche in life or are making a career choice, it would be helpful to look into your Mercury placement to see where you shine. It may also tell you about your communication style, so it's interesting to compare this placement with the Mercury of your partner to see how your dynamics will work in a confrontation.

For example, someone whose Mercury is in Leo will probably have an easy time navigating social drama and playing cheerleader for both themselves and others. They're very good at compliments and flattery; they know what they would like to hear, so they say that to others to make them feel good! Similarly, someone with their Mercury in Scorpio has an innate ability to understand how words affect people, so they're very good at phrasing things carefully and using words to their advantage. Taurus Mercuries have a firm grasp on logic and common sense because they have access to Taurus's grounded and stubborn decision-making processes.

Venus

When you're comparing your natal chart with your crush's, don't look at your Sun sign to judge your compatibility; instead, look at your Venus! As the ruler of Taurus and Libra, Venus symbolizes our love life, sense of beauty, and what attracts us. It can also reveal our long-term goals for love, such as whether we're looking to make a family or if we're just looking for a good time. Venus may also give us details about other aspects of our social lives, such as the things we look for in friendships and the sorts of people we are immediately drawn to in a crowd of strangers. And, since it determines our sense of beauty, our preference for certain clothing styles could be affected by our Venus placement. If you didn't relate to the styles listed under your Rising sign, perhaps your Venus is particularly powerful and has influenced your taste in fashion!

Aries is a competitive sign that craves excitement, so someone with an Aries Venus definitely enjoys chasing (or being chased!) at the start of a relationship. They will also need plenty of fun when the relationship is more settled to ensure that they stay interested. On the reverse end of the spectrum, an anxious Cancer would prefer to be with someone who can give them a sense of security. A Cancer Venus will only date those with whom they feel they could start a family, and they aren't going to risk heartbreak. The optimistic and fun Sagittarius is always looking for a good time, so a Sagittarius Venus will be attracted to someone who can make them laugh and who can take them on fun trips.

Mars

Mars, the ruler of Aries, symbolizes all the parts of humanity that are still animalistic and primal. It's our survival instinct, aggression, and energy. Our Mars placement tells us the sorts of things that get us worked up, and it also tells us how we behave once we've been angered. Although many people treat Mars as though it only controls our aggression, this sign also works in tandem with Venus to describe the other half of our romantic life. While Venus shows us what we're attracted to and what we think is beautiful, our Mars placements tell us about our more primal desires, sexual urges, and physical chemistry. If you want to know whether you're compatible with someone for a one-night stand rather than a long-term relationship, looking to your Mars placements may be a better bet than just your Venus.

Someone with a Gemini Mars is in need of constant stimulation in order to feel engaged, focused, and to perform their best. They probably have to jump from task to task quickly if they want to complete anything on their to-do list. They also need to spice things up in their relationships often, especially in the bedroom. Meanwhile, someone with their Mars in Libra gets extremely worked up if they're forced to pick a side in a situation or argument, especially if they would much rather stay neutral on the issue. They hate seeing things in black-and-white and may get angry when grey is not an option. Mars in Capricorn sometimes feels an instinctual need for control, but if they can keep a reign on that urge, they are capable of using their anger to fuel action, planning, and change.

Jupiter

Jupiter symbolizes our hopes, dreams, and potential for expansion. It's no wonder that the Sagittarius is so optimistic with a planet like Jupiter as its ruler! By looking at our Jupiter placement, we learn a bit more about our hidden skills and the sorts of behaviors that will help us make progress in life. Jupiter also gives us the passion we need to pursue money and become skilled at our jobs, so you may see a lot of the things that make you excited and motivated reflected in your Jupiter placement as well. Jupiter isn't always positive, however. This sign also tells us the sort of things that may make us conceitful or self-centered if we have too much of it. If you're ever wondering why an unpleasant person acts the way they do, their Jupiter sign *might* explain a lot of their behavior!

For instance, someone with their Jupiter in Aquarius is motivated by things that are odd or unusual. They might want to try something just because it hasn't been tried beforehand. They're blessed with a natural curiosity and an extremely open mind. However, they must watch themselves to ensure that they don't think they're more special than other people because of this uniqueness. Someone with their Jupiter in Cancer would be highly motivated by a need to care for others or be fair to other people, so they perform well in their jobs when they feel that fairness is on the line. However, if they become too caught-up in this endeavor, they can be unwilling to change and try new things. Lastly, Jupiter in Aries is motivated by competition, opportunities to learn, and chances for leadership. They would adore *any* job where there's a possibility of climbing the ranks. They may also be prone to risky behaviors or starting too many projects at once without finishing any of them.

Saturn

Saturn, ruler of the disciplined Capricorn, symbolizes law, responsibility, and ambition. It's also a very grounded planet and tells us about the reality of our lives. It often illustrates the sorts of obstacles that we are going to face, the kinds of questions we need to ask ourselves, and more. Saturn is always a very helpful teacher. Regardless of where we are in life or what we're aiming to do, looking to our Saturn placement can be beneficial for our overall growth. Once you know the lesson that Saturn has for you, you will certainly see great improvements in your life and will be ready to tackle the next adventure! It may not be easy, especially since Saturn tends to ask big, philosophical questions, but it will be worth it!

If your Saturn is in Pisces, then being emotionally open may be a challenge for you. Although all of your friends and peers turn to you for emotional guidance, you have a hard time asking for help yourself. Saturn is trying to encourage you to open up and accept the help you deserve. Leo is fun-loving, so someone with their Saturn in Leo may have had a lot of trouble having fun in the past. Perhaps they had to grow up too quickly or were bullied for the things that gave them pleasure. Saturn wants you to reconnect with your inner child and learn to have fun again! Taurus loves material possessions and are the most comforted when they are surrounded by beautiful things. Someone with their Saturn in Taurus may either have no materialistic tendencies at all and are being challenged to pamper themselves a little, or they are too attached to money and define their worth based on how much wealth they accumulate. If that's the case, Saturn wants them to realize that they are worth more than their bank accounts.

Uranus

Uranus, the ruler of futuristic Aquarius, symbolizes unpredictable changes and sudden occurrences. Uranus changes its course very slowly, so it often predicts generational changes rather than personal ones. For instance, Uranus will be in Taurus from 2021 until 2026. However, we can still look at Uranus in our charts to see how our individual lives are affected by sudden changes. Uranus is the *perfect* placement for those who like to plan or who are looking to predict the future; it tells us all about the unexpected, and about major upcoming trends. Astrologers in the past have used its position to foretell the creation of new technologies, and more!

Everyone born between 1995 and 2003 have their Uranus in Aquarius. This comes as no surprise; Aquarius is forward-thinking and creative, and the people born between these years have never known a time without the internet. They also tend to have more progressive ideals and are always thinking about the future and humanity as a whole. Uranus was in Sagittarius from 1981 to 1988. Sagittarius is a trailblazer and so are the people born in this time. They contain the bulk of the older millennials who have been reshaping our educational systems and reject the nine-to-five job schedule. And, during the years 2003 to 2011, when Uranus was in Pisces, the world was having more open discussions about healing, mental health, and spirituality. Seems fitting for the soft, spiritually-attuned Pisces!

Neptune

Neptune, the ruler of Pisces, is the planet of dreams, delusions, and inspiration. It has a large effect on the arts, including dance, music, and poetry, and its rotation has corresponded with a lot of art movements throughout history. Neptune moves extremely slowly; it takes about 146 years to cycle through the 12 zodiacs and spends approximately 14 years in each. Neptune is currently in its native sign of Pisces, where it's been since 2011 and will stay until 2025. This means that many people during this time may be resorting to escapism as a way to deal with reality, which makes sense with the recent improvements in video games, movie graphics, and more. After that, it will move into Aries, which foretells that people will become more assertive about their beliefs and will be more willing to stand up for what's right. Art may also take a new form and become more "in your face", so to speak.

Pluto

Pluto, the ruler of Scorpio, was actually only discovered in 1930 and was demoted to "dwarf planet" in 2006, but astrologers maintain that its gravitational pull is strong enough to still affect the zodiac and the way we understand astrology. Pluto is a planet of power, and it gives a lot of strength to whatever sign it's in at that time. For instance, Pluto was in Sagittarius from 1995 to 2006, and it had extra influence on all of the other fire signs as well. During that time, there were a lot of falsehoods and lies being burned away as well as an emergence of new truths. This is related to Sagittarius's natural curiosity and desire for knowledge. Since that time, Pluto has been in Capricorn and will stay there until 2024. The last time Pluto was here, it was during the American Revolution, when people emphasized the "pursuit of happiness" and placed a great emphasis on an individual's freedom and desires. Since then, happiness has been hard to find, and Pluto is once again illustrating how unhappy people have been in our current systems. Here, Capricorn's discipline has been a negative thing, and Pluto is drawing this to our attention.

Other Celestial Bodies

There's more in our skies than just the Sun and the other planets in our solar system! Our universe is huge and contains an enormous number of different objects in it, and some of these are close enough to be considered when we're interpreting a zodiac. Not only that, but there are certain mathematical points such as the 'Lilith' that are used to determine certain qualities of our personalities.

Lilith

This mysterious sign isn't actually indicative of a physical landmark at all. Instead, it's a mathematical point that's related to the cycle of the Moon. The Moon travels in an elliptical shape around the Earth, meaning that sometimes it's quite far away from us, and sometimes, it's significantly closer. Regardless of the Moon's location, we can calculate where it's furthest point, referred to as the *apogee*, would be. Wherever that point lies, that's called our 'Lilith' or sometimes our "Black Moon". Its placement tells us where we really shine and are able to go our own way, as opposed to following the crowd. For instance, those with their Lilith in Virgo are always ready for disaster and are capable of acting independently where others might be frozen in place. If their Lilith is in Capricorn, they are able to act as leaders and don't need any advisors or right-hand men to help them make decisions while they're at the top. And, if their Lilith is in Pisces, they can listen to their dreams and intuitions even if the whole world is telling them that they're wrong.

Comets

These celestial bodies are sometimes very unpredictable, so it's difficult to tell *exactly* what their influence will be. However, some studies held by astrologers of particular comets, such as Panstarrs, tells us that they usually bring a drastic, unforeseen shock. Panstarrs flew from Aquarius to Pisces and disappeared in Aries between the days of February 12 and March 9 of 2013, and a number of shocking events occurred during that time. North Korea and South Korea ceased cooperation, Pope Benedict XVI resigned, and a meteor struck Russia and left 1,400 people injured. This is a pattern for multiple comets, as well. The Suez Crisis began when the comet "Arend-Roland" was in our skies in 1957, which was also the year that Osama bin Laden was born. Many of the in-depth natal chart calculators that you find online will include the locations of major comets and may even give you a description of what astrologers assume its appearance means in your chart, but as a general rule, we believe that those born while a comet is in the sky are innovative thinkers who are not resistant to change, are good under pressure, and are willing to accept more progressive views.

Stars

There are about 5,000 visible stars in our night sky, and some astrologers use up to 100 of them as they make predictions or create detailed natal charts. These stars typically represent different things and are used if their relationship with another placement in the chart is notable or stands out in any way. For example, the star 'Aldebaran' is the dominant star in the Taurus constellation and is an indicator of fame, fortune, and popularity, but could predict a violent death. John F. Kennedy had Aldebaran in a conjunct position to his Sun, and his son, John F. Kennedy Jr., had it in his Rising sign. Both of them had violent, gruesome deaths, but enjoyed fame during their lifetimes. 'Antares' is the alpha star in Sagittarius, and is indicative of an adventurous spirit and courage, but is also a sign of multiple marriages, sudden loss, and injury to the eyes. Brittney Spears, Woody Allen, and Bette Midler all have Antares conjunct their Sun signs.

Chapter 5: Using the Zodiac

Now that you understand what the various placements and the 12 signs represent, you may be feeling ready to use that knowledge to your advantage. The zodiac is more than just a personality test or a cool trick to pull out at parties; it can also be a tool that assists you at various points of your life. Whether you're looking to pursue a new love, apply to different jobs, or you're just looking for a way to improve your everyday life, astrology has an answer for you. I will be covering a number of different methods to take advantage of your new astrological knowledge in simple ways that are accessible to the beginner. Namely, I will discuss the use of crystals, basic concepts of sign compatibility, and timing-related concepts such as Returns and Retrogrades.

Crystals

Even if you're only *just* beginning your spiritual journey, you may have already heard about the magical powers of crystals. Crystals and stones are *huge* energy-magnets, and they can be used to help you attract a specific energy that you want. Keeping a crystal in your pocket, by your bed, or using it as a meditation tool is a fantastic way to manifest your desires. You can choose specific crystals according to your wants at the time, or you can balance your overall energies by choosing a crystal that resonates with your zodiac sign. When you're doing this, you can use your Sun placement for an overall improvement, or you can target a different placement by choosing a stone that works best for it. Have your emotions been unpredictable? Perhaps you should try balancing your Moon placement!

- **Aries**: An Aries who has lost their fire is depressed, anxious, and often quite fatigued. To help reignite this sign, try red stones like carnelian and red jasper or stones with a lot of solar energy, like citrine.

- **Taurus**: Tauruses are at their best when their energy is calm and collected rather than stubborn and hardheaded. Stones that keep them relaxed, such as amazonite, selenite, and smoky quartz, will help them feel amazing.

- **Gemini**: Although this sign is extroverted and bubbly, sometimes their minds move too quickly and make them prone to extreme anxiety. Some crystals that can ease this are shungite, amazonite, and tiger's eye.

- **Cancer**: Cancers are so empathetic and sensitive that they are strongly affected by negativity, so they need stones that protect their energies. Some good options are selenite, labradorite, and red jasper.

- **Leo**: The prideful, dramatic Leo is prone to getting their head too far in the clouds and losing sight of reality. To prevent this, grounding stones like tiger's eye, rose quartz, and garnet will ensure that they stay connected to others.

- **Virgo**: Virgos are often caught up in their perfectionism and need a reminder that they can be content with the way things are. Stones like amazonite, amethyst, and fluorite can help them with that.

- **Libra**: Libras feel their best when they're surrounded by adventure and laughter, so they work well with stones that help them feel secure as they pursue new things. Tiger's eye, amethyst, and bloodstone could be good fits.

- **Scorpio**: Being both determined and sensitive, a Scorpio could use some help keeping their energy balanced and making sure that they can stay *exactly* as independent as they want to be. Stones like pink tourmaline, amethyst, and K2 can provide that for them.

- **Sagittarius**: As lovers of adventure, travel, and experiences, burnout is the Sagittarius's worst enemy.

They work best with stones that replenish and protect them, such as lepidolite, smoky quartz, and shungite.

- **Capricorn**: Capricorns are *always* striving to be the best, achieve everything they want in life, and do it all in style. They can also be very hard on themselves if they can't do all of it *perfectly*, so self-love stones like rose quartz, garnet, and smoky quartz will help them immensely.

- **Aquarius**: The Aquarius is always looking to the future, and while that's often a good thing, they can become unbalanced and lose sight of the present. They will appreciate stones that are grounding but still keep them attached to their higher selves, like lepidolite, amethyst, and tourmalinated quartz.

- **Pisces**: Pisces, like Sagittarius, are at risk for burnout, but in an emotional and spiritual sense. They need crystals that help them keep their energy high while also still expressing themselves, like clear quartz, carnelian, and chrysocolla.

Compatibility

A lot of people first start exploring astrology specifically because they want to learn how to judge the compatibility between people. Whether they're looking for a new love, friends, or are wondering how well they'll get along with their coworkers, it's sometimes hard to navigate social situations, and astrology can certainly be a helpful tool. Remember that just using your Sun sign isn't *always* helpful when judging compatibility; look to your Venus signs for an overall love reading and your Mars if you're curious about the bedroom. For more platonic relationships, your Moon signs may be particularly relevant as well. Remember, too, that the zodiac *isn't* written in stone. If two people are determined to make a relationship work, it *can* usually work! With that said, here are the basic compatibilities between signs:

- **Aries**: Most compatible with Gemini and Aquarius, least compatible with Cancer and Capricorn.

- **Taurus**: Most compatible with Cancer and Pisces, least compatible with Leo and Aquarius.

- **Gemini**: Most compatible with Aries and Leo, least compatible with Virgo and Pisces.

- **Cancer**: Most compatible with Taurus and Virgo, least compatible with Aries and Libra.

- **Leo**: Most compatible with Gemini and Libra, least compatible with Scorpio and Taurus.

- **Virgo**: Most compatible with Cancer and Scorpio, least compatible with Gemini and Sagittarius.

- **Libra**: Most compatible with Leo and Sagittarius, least compatible with Cancer and Capricorn.

- **Scorpio**: Most compatible with Virgo and Capricorn, least compatible with Leo and Aquarius.

- **Sagittarius**: Most compatible with Libra and Aquarius, least compatible with Virgo and Pisces.

- **Capricorn**: Most compatible with Scorpio and Pisces, least compatible with Aries and Libra.

- **Aquarius**: Most compatible with Aries and Sagittarius, least compatible with Taurus and Scorpio.

- **Pisces**: Most compatible with Taurus and Capricorn, least compatible with Gemini and Sagittarius.

Planetary Returns

Since the planets move in a cycle, there comes multiple points in your life where a planet returns to the exact same position it was in on the day that you were born. In astrology, those moments are referred to as a 'Return', and they bear a number of mystical properties depending on what planet is making the return. In general, they represent new starts, a chance for growth, or a new opportunity. Think of them as another birth for whatever aspect of life the planet symbolizes. Returns are especially helpful for anyone who uses astrology because they help you decide the best time to pursue new things. Do you want to start dating again but can't figure out when would be the right time? Maybe you should wait until your Venus Return before you redownload that dating app.

Some returns happen very frequently, such as the "Lunar Return". This occurs once a month. Others are monthly too, such as the Sun, Mercury, and Venus. Others take multiple years to occur. The often-feared "Saturn Return", for example, only happens every 29.5 years while our Jupiter Return will be every 12-13 years.

Let's discuss the individual effects of each Return. The Solar Return occurs once a year around the month of your birthday. Do you ever feel yourself more willing to try new things or make new goals around your birthday? That's because the Sun is granting you a chance to recreate your life once it's back in your season. Your Lunar Return happens 13 times a year when the Moon reenters the same phase it was in when you were born. It can be a good chance to 'reset' your default emotion and set the theme for the upcoming month. Your Mercury Return occurs once a year and is typically around the same time as your birthday, but usually not the same day. It foresees a new communication style, mode of expressing ourselves, and chances to gain knowledge. The Venus Return is also once a year, but can be very far from our birthdays. It's the best time to seek new relationships of both romantic and platonic natures. The Mars Return is every 1.5-2 years and can symbolize the change of passions, hobbies, and motivations. Our first Jupiter Return occurs at the start of puberty, and it usually comes with major milestones, growth, and developments. The dreaded "Saturn Return" comes at points in our lives when we tend to reevaluate where we're heading and take ourselves seriously, such as when we're about to enter our 30s and when we're entering our 60s.

If you want to take advantage of your Returns and be prepared for them, you can calculate your Return chart. It's similar to a natal chart but contains specific information as to *when* the planets will go back to the positions they held at your birth.

Planetary Retrogrades

"Planetary Retrogrades" are perhaps the most feared and misunderstood parts of astrology. When someone hears that a planet is in 'retrograde', regardless of what the planet is, everyone assumes that their life is going to go topsy-turvy until that retrograde is over. Although some retrogrades *can* get a little crazy, they aren't as bad as many people think. A 'retrograde' occurs when a planet appears to be moving backwards from our perspective here on Earth. Of course, planets don't *actually* move backwards. It's an illusion caused by the pattern of their cycle. Imagine standing at the starting line of a race, and when the whistle blows, the person next to you takes off way faster than you do. For a mere moment, you might feel as though you're moving backwards, but it's only because your speed differs from the speed of the other person. *That's* a retrograde; no one is *really* moving backwards, but it gets confusing.

Retrogrades affect us in a similar way. During the time of a retrograde, life may throw a particular challenge at us that makes us feel as though we are moving backwards and losing progress. Don't let it discourage you; it's actually progress in disguise. You will learn from that challenge and be able to make progress even more effectively after it's handled. A retrograde may also be a good time to reflect on the past and remember the lessons you've learned thus far.

The Sun and Moon *never* retrograde, but the other planets do, and it happens at varying rates. The "Mercury Retrograde" is definitely the most famous, and it occurs three to four times a year and lasts about three weeks each time it happens. Although Mercury usually encourages us to start new things, its retrograde is a sign to stay still, evaluate what you've done so far, and reflect. Don't make any impulse decisions; they will certainly backfire! The "Venus Retrograde" that occurs once every 18 months is a chance to reflect on our relationships and move on from old ones, and the "Mars Retrograde" once every 2-2.5 years will help you reevaluate where you're placing your energy. The same message applies to the rest of the planets; they bear the opposite meaning during a retrograde, but that doesn't necessarily mean they're negative!

Conclusion

Thank you for taking the time to learn a little bit more about astrology!

By now, you will have a good fundamental understanding of the different Sun, Moon, and Rising signs, and what impact each of them has on our personalities and temperaments.

Through reading this book you should have also gained a greater understanding of those around you, and how best to interact with them based on their astrological signs. Further to that, you'll have discovered which people you're most compatible with in regard to both romantic relationships and friendships.

Thank you once again for taking the time to learn all about astrology. I wish you the best of luck on your spiritual journey!

References

Astrology. (n.d.). In *Cambridge Dictionary*. https://dictionary.cambridge.org/us/dictionary/english/astrology.

Astrology Planets and their Meanings, Planet Symbols and Cheat Sheet. (2018, January 27). Labyrinthos. https://labyrinthos.co/blogs/astrology-horoscope-zodiac-signs/astrology-planets-and-their-meanings-planet-symbols-and-cheat-sheet

Astrology: Celtic Symbols and Irish Astrology. (2013, January 2). Apanache. https://a-panache.com/irish-claddagh-ring/irish-astrology-symbols/

Brown, M. (2020, September 25). *What Your Moon Sign Means About Your Personality and Life Path*. Shape. https://www.shape.com/lifestyle/mind-and-body/moon-sign-meaning

Brown, M. (2021, February 3). *How to Use Astrology to Judge Your Romantic — and Sexual — Compatibility*. Shape. https://www.shape.com/lifestyle/sex-and-love/astrology-zodiac-signs-compatibility

Campbell, S. (2020, July 8). *A Guide To What Retrograde Actually Means & How Each Planet's Retrograde*

Affects You. StyleCaster.
https://stylecaster.com/feature/what-does-retrograde-
mean-1134829/

Chang, R. (2014, October 30). *Comets in Astrology*.
Www.astro.com.
https://www.astro.com/astrology/aa_article141030_e.h
tm

Christoforou, P. (2016, February 13). *How do Astronomy and
Astrology Differ?* Astronomy Trek.
https://www.astronomytrek.com/how-do-astronomy-
and-astrology-differ/

Faragher, A. K. (2019, December 19). *What the Position of
Venus in Your Birth Chart Means for You*. Allure.
https://www.allure.com/story/venus-birth-chart-planet-
of-love

Gat, A., David, S., & Bolen, A. (2019, September 11). *Mercury in
the Signs: What Your Mercury Placement Means For
You*. Www.vice.com.
https://www.vice.com/en/article/8xwx3v/what-does-
mercury-in-the-signs-mean-in-my-birth-chart

Geddes, L. (2019, July 31). *The mood-altering power of the
Moon*. Www.bbc.com.

https://www.bbc.com/future/article/20190731-is-the-moon-impacting-your-mood-and-wellbeing

Geller, L. (2019, June 13). *Why Knowing Your Mars Sign Might Help You Control Your Anger*. Women's Health. https://www.womenshealthmag.com/life/g27912214/mars-sign/?slide=10

Ghaneh, I. (2008, July 14). *What To Expect Astrologically Under Pluto In Capricorn*. Llewellyn Worldwide. https://www.llewellyn.com/journal/article/1566

Grabianowski, E. (2005, May 26). *What is Astrology?* HowStuffWorks. https://entertainment.howstuffworks.com/horoscopes-astrology/question749.htm

Halsted, N. (2020, July 30). *Here's What Your Rising Sign Says About Your Appearance, According To Medical Astrology*. Thought Catalog. https://thoughtcatalog.com/nikki-halsted/2020/07/heres-what-your-rising-sign-says-about-your-appearance-according-to-medical-astrology/

Houlding, D. (n.d.). *Skyscript: The Life & Work of Ptolemy by Deborah Houlding*. Www.skyscript.co.uk. http://www.skyscript.co.uk/ptolemy.html

Jarus, O. (2017, September 8). *Ancient Babylon: Center of Mesopotamian Civilization*. Live Science. https://www.livescience.com/28701-ancient-babylon-center-of-mesopotamian-civilization.html

Keene, B. (2019, May 17). *Written in the Stars: Astronomy and Astrology in Medieval Manuscripts*. Brewminate. https://brewminate.com/written-in-the-stars-astronomy-and-astrology-in-medieval-manuscripts/

Lantz, P. (n.d.). *Stars in Astrology*. LoveToKnow. https://horoscopes.lovetoknow.com/astrology-signs-personality/stars-astrology

Miller, S. (n.d.). *Neptune*. Susan Miller Astrology Zone. https://www.astrologyzone.com/learn-astrology/the-planets/neptune/

Ourisman, J. (2020, July 30). *The Best Crystals for Your Zodiac Sign, According to an Expert*. FabFitFun. https://fabfitfun.com/magazine/crystals-for-your-zodiac-sign/

Planetary Returns. (n.d.). Horoscope.com. https://www.horoscope.com/astrology/returns/

Roberts, T. (2014, July 11). *Jupiter – Meaning and Influence in Astrology*. Insightful Psychics.

https://www.insightfulpsychics.com/jupiter-planets-astrology/

Sesay, A. (2020, October 20). *Your Saturn Sign Is Your Cosmic Teacher—Here's How to Find Yours*. Cosmopolitan. https://www.cosmopolitan.com/lifestyle/a34426595/saturn-sign-meaning/

Sesay, A. (2021, March 9). *Your Uranus Sign Knows How You'll Change the World*. Cosmopolitan. https://www.cosmopolitan.com/lifestyle/a35716192/uranus-sign-meaning/

Simone, E. (2019, November 12). *Here's How to Find Your Rising Sign in Astrology*. Allure. https://www.allure.com/story/rising-sign-personality-traits-astrology-ascendant-signs

Temming, M. (2014, July 14). *Astrology vs Astronomy: What's the Difference?* Sky & Telescope. https://skyandtelescope.org/astronomy-resources/whats-difference-astrology-vs-astronomy/

The 12 Animals of the Chinese Zodiac. (n.d.). Mandarinhouse.com. https://mandarinhouse.com/12-animals-of-the-chinese-zodiac

The Sun in Astrology, The Zodiac. (n.d.). Cafeastrology.com. https://cafeastrology.com/sun.html

Theodoros Karasavvas. (2017, April 9). *The 4,000 Year History of Horoscopes: How Astrology Has Been Shaped Throughout the Millennia*. Ancient-Origins.net; Ancient Origins. https://www.ancient-origins.net/history-ancient-traditions/4000-year-history-horoscopes-how-astrology-has-been-shaped-throughout-021321

Weaver, S. (n.d.). *Astrology Careers by Sun Sign | Metaphorical Platypus*. https://www.metaphoricalplatypus.com/fun-stuff/astrology/astrology-careers-by-sun-sign/

Wright, J. (2020, December 30). *What Your Lilith Sign (Aka Your Inner B*tch) Says About You*. PureWow. https://www.purewow.com/wellness/lilith-sign

Zodiac Signs. (2021). Costarastrology.com. https://www.costarastrology.com/zodiac-signs/

www.ingramcontent.com/pod-product-compliance
Lightning Source LLC
Chambersburg PA
CBHW071116120626
46546CB00003B/1360